IT'S NOT BUSINESS,
IT'S PERSONAL

BOB SORGE

Oasis House
Kansas City, Missouri

Other books by Bob Sorge:
•*POWER OF THE BLOOD: Approaching God With Confidence*
•*UNRELENTING PRAYER*
•*LOYALTY: The Reach Of The Noble Heart*
•*FOLLOWING THE RIVER: A Vision For Corporate Worship*
•*ENVY: The Enemy Within*
•*SECRETS OF THE SECRET PLACE*
•*Secrets Of The Secret Place COMPANION STUDY GUIDE*
•*GLORY: When Heaven Invades Earth*
•*DEALING WITH THE REJECTION AND PRAISE OF MAN*
•*PAIN, PERPLEXITY, AND PROMOTION: A prophetic interpretation of the
book of Job*
•*THE FIRE OF GOD'S LOVE*
•*THE FIRE OF DELAYED ANSWERS*
•*IN HIS FACE: A prophetic call to renewed focus*
•*EXPLORING WORSHIP: A practical guide to praise and worship*
•*Exploring Worship WORKBOOK & DISCUSSION GUIDE*
•*THE CHASTENING OF THE LORD (later in 2009/2010)*
(see the Order Form at the back of this book)

IT'S NOT BUSINESS, IT'S PERSONAL
Copyright © 2009 by Bob Sorge
Published by Oasis House
PO Box 522
Grandview, MO 64030-0522

www.oasishouse.net

All Scripture quotations are from the New King James Version of the
Bible. Copyright © 1979, 1980, 1982, Thomas Nelson Inc., Publisher.
Used by permission.

Edited by Edie Veach.

Printed in the United States of America
International Standard Book Number: 978-0-9749664-6-5

DEDICATION

To Joel, my son.

Joel, you have chosen the place of standing before the Bridegroom and hearing His voice. You have opted for a fasted lifestyle because over and over, when decisions were placed before you, you have chosen in favor of personal devotion to Jesus.

I dedicate this book to you because its message is the reach of your soul.

I'm proud of you and of the nurturing environment you and Anna are providing my grandchildren.

With all my affections,

Dad.

CONTENTS

CHAPTER 1

JESUS AND HIS
BRIDE

I'm reluctant to admit it, but I got the title for this book from a movie.

Sometimes you'll find a one-liner in a movie that will arrest your attention with its profundity. That's what happened to me while watching the movie, *You've Got Mail*. I'll paint the backdrop so the one-liner makes sense.

In the movie, Meg Ryan plays the role of a bookshop owner in New York City who inherits the business from her mother. With her mother now deceased, the bookshop means the universe to Meg. It's her inheritance, her livelihood, her passion, her future. Her entire world revolves around this bookshop.

Tom Hanks plays the other main character in the movie. He's a multi-millionaire who owns a chain of book superstores, and he decides to open one of his superstores right around the corner from Meg's tiny bookshop. That development incites Meg to try to save her livelihood by launching a campaign of negative publicity against Hanks and his superstore.

The plot has an interesting twist to it. Hanks and Ryan,

totally by chance, happen to strike an anonymous friendship through email correspondence. Without realizing who he's emailing, Hanks begins to give Ryan counsel (via email) on how to deal with the person who is making problems for her business. He encourages her to resist her competitor with everything she's got. To bolster her confidence, he keeps repeating his mantra, "It's not personal, it's business." What he means is, when you attack your competitor, you're not launching an attack against him personally; you're merely making wise business moves. Be combative. Put up a fight. There's nothing personal about what you're doing; it's strictly what must be done to survive in the business world.

He tells her to keep repeating to herself, "It's not personal, it's business."

Soon thereafter, Hanks learns of the true identity of the woman he's been emailing. She's the owner of the bookshop that he's putting out of business! As the irony of it strikes him, something else also strikes him: He's falling in love with her!

Hanks begins to spend more time with Ryan, purposely finding ways to get to know her better. Throughout their budding friendship, Hanks knows that he's emailing Ryan, but Ryan doesn't know she's meeting with the man whom she is anonymously emailing.

Well, the inevitable happens. Meg Ryan's customer activity plummets, and she is forced to close her business.

After Meg's business dies, Tom Hanks has a sudden epiphany and realizes he wants to marry Meg. But how can he possibly win her heart, now that he's the one responsible for putting her out of business?

It's against this backdrop that we come to a scene in the movie in which Tom and Meg are together and Tom is trying to formulate an apology for putting her out of business. What can he say? At a loss for words, he reverts to his old slogan and lamely says to her, "It wasn't personal."

Meg's response is classic. "All that means, is that it wasn't personal to you. But it was personal to me. Because whatever else anything is, it ought to *begin* by being personal." At that, Tom Hanks is rendered entirely speechless.

IT'S PERSONAL TO JESUS

The profundity of Meg's response is amazingly applicable to the church of Jesus Christ. To Jesus, the church is not a business. It's personal.

Jesus is not merely an astute businessman who has found a promising enterprise on one of His planets. He's not an entrepreneur who is working a new angle to enlarge His inheritance. He's not a speculator who is trying His hand at a new, innovative venture. No, none of these images come even close to depicting the heart of Jesus and His mission on planet Earth.

Rather, Jesus is a lovesick Bridegroom who has come to win the affections of a Bride—the Bride His Father has promised Him.

Love isn't business, it's personal.

Allow me, therefore, to take Tom Hanks's mantra, invert the wording, and make this statement regarding Jesus' perspective on the church:

It's not business, it's personal.

A METAPHOR FROM MARRIAGE

Jesus has a vested interest in the church. We're called His espoused Bride, or in today's lingo, His Fiancée. The wedding day hasn't happened yet, but it's fast approaching.

We're not a business acquisition that He is seeking to conquer; rather, we're an eternal soul mate He is seeking to woo. He's after a lovesick Bride. That makes it personal.

As someone who was once a bridegroom, I can relate. On my wedding day, I did not enter into the marriage covenant with my wife, Marci, as though it were a business venture. I was *not* thinking to myself, "She's got good teeth, a strong back, and plenty of grit. She's going to make my bed, cook my meals, mend my clothes, iron my shirts, clean my floors, buy my groceries, give me children, and manage my household."

Now, as it turns out, she does *all* those things. A marriage, rightly expressed, means that both spouses labor side by side to complete all the tasks necessary to make life work. When I'm out of town on a trip, for example, I'm totally grateful that I can relax regarding the home front, knowing that Marci is keeping all the wheels of our household machinery running smoothly and efficiently.

But that's not why I married her. I married her for but one reason: love. I knew there would be a lot of responsibilities to tend to in our new household and that she would help me according to her abilities; but bottom line, I didn't marry a business partner, I married a lover.

The same is true for Jesus. He didn't die on the cross to procure a helper for His household chores. The abject horror and extravagant abandonment of the cross were not endured merely for the sake of winning a domestic maid. No, He died to gain for Himself a lover, a companion, a Bride.

He did the cross for love.

The very reason this is all personal to Jesus is because of the cross. When He endured the cross, that made this whole thing profoundly personal. There's nothing more personal than when you're hanging on a tree. (When they put nails in your hands, you take it personally.) Jesus' relationship with us became, in those six hours of suffering, as personal as the cross itself. It was a personal cross, and it's a personal Bride.

Furthermore, Jesus didn't come simply to recruit an army (as though He needed warriors—He already had plenty within the hosts of heaven). He wasn't looking to marry a crusty battle-ax-of-a-woman who would intimidate His enemies with her brawn. True, we will ride forth with Him to do battle at the end of the age against the antichrist and his armies (Revelation 19); but our primary identity will not be that of a warrior but of a Bride. The final metaphor the Bible uses to identify us is that of a Bride (see Revelation 22:17).

THE LINE BETWEEN BUSINESS AND PERSONAL

When a man's in business, he *expects* other businessmen to compete with him. He's not offended when another entrepreneur tries to under-bid him or out-produce him. They can place quotations on the same contract they're both trying to land, and then go to lunch together. Their relationship is cordial because it's understood that competition is an intrinsic element of business.

If the other guy makes a play for your wife, however, now *that's* an altogether different matter! Now it's no longer business; now it's personal!

If you incur a man's jealousy by committing adultery with his wife, you can try to satisfy him by offering him cash, but it will be to no avail. No amount of money will appease a husband's fury because the whole ordeal is not business, it's personal.

For a man, the lines between business and personal are very clear. He might take his wife on a business trip, and during the day be entirely absorbed in his professional dealings.

But when dusk settles in and it's time to take his wife to dinner, the business is completely set aside and the evening takes on a relaxed, intimate ambience. Because when it comes to things like wife and children and close family, it's not business, it's personal.

THERE *Is* KINGDOM BUSINESS TO DO

To paint a complete picture, I need to make clear that there *are* elements to the Kingdom that are business in nature. After all, it was Jesus who said, "'Do business till I come'" (Luke 19:13). Somebody has to formulate and manage church budgets. We must organize events and administrate people. Sometimes we find ourselves constructing new buildings to accommodate Kingdom activities. Distributing food and clothing effectively to the poor requires a good business head. The business of the Kingdom involves calendars, people, schedules, cars, buses, airplanes, purchases, meetings, meals, offices, equipment, phones, emails, banks, etc. But even while we're doing all the necessary business of the Kingdom, we're constantly reminding ourselves that we're doing it because of the affectionate relationship we have with God through our Lord Jesus Christ.

Jesus Himself is an outstanding businessman, actually. And He's not interested in doing it all solo. He likes it when His Bride is at His side, doing stuff with Him. There's all *kinds* of things He's planning on doing with her. He has plans for her to rule and reign with Him forever on the earth (Revelation 5:10). He has plans for her to judge angels and kings (1 Corinthians 6:2-3; Revelation 2:26-27; 20:4), and reclaim the stewardship and dominion of man over all the earth (Genesis 1:28). She is going to be incredibly active, both during the 1,000-year reign of Christ on the earth, and thereafter in the eternal state. There's a *whole lot* they're going to do together!

But more than anything else, Jesus wants it to be about love. He wants our partnering labors with Him to flow out of the intimacy of burning, fiery lovesickness. The loving relationship is always the primary delight; the working relationship is an overflow of that intimacy (see Matthew 22:27-29).

CHAPTER 2

THE FRIEND
OF THE BRIDEGROOM

John the Baptist had supernatural revelation into the identity of God's people as a Bride. He was shown by the
Holy Spirit that Jesus was a heavenly Bridegroom who had
come to earth for a Bride. He was also given divine insight
into the nature of his role in serving that holy romance.

In talking to his disciples about it, John told them that
he had a unique relationship to Jesus. He called himself "the
friend of the bridegroom." By using this phrase, John cap-
tured in a single image both the personal nature of the relationship between the Bride and the Bridegroom as well as
the personal nature of the relationship between himself and
the Bridegroom.

> *"He who has the bride is the bridegroom; but the friend
> of the bridegroom, who stands and hears him, rejoices
> greatly because of the bridegroom's voice. Therefore
> this joy of mine is fulfilled"* (John 3:29).

John painted an allegorical picture for us in this verse.
The covenant people of God are depicted as "the bride"; the
Messiah who was coming to deliver them is called "the bride-
groom"; and John himself is "the friend of the bridegroom."

In today's wedding lingo, we would call John "the best man."

In one verse, John painted a word picture that comprises for us perhaps the most compelling revelation in all of Scripture of the kind of relationship Jesus wants to have with His ministers and servants. As we serve His Bride, He wants our relationship with Him to be that of friendship, not employment.

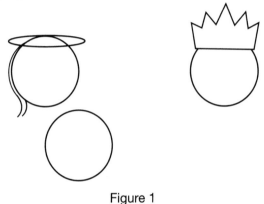

Figure 1

The above figure demonstrates John's allegory. The Bridegroom on the right is Jesus, the Bride on the left is the covenant people of God, and next to the Bride stands John, the friend of the Bridegroom. You'll notice the span between the Bridegroom and the Bride. That span is meant to portray the long-distance relationship the Bride had with the Bridegroom prior to His coming. Prior to His arrival, the friend of the Groom stood at the Bride's side to serve her.

The friend was sent ahead of time by the Bridegroom to prepare the Bride for His coming. As the Groom's friend, it was John's job to get the Bride's heart ready for her Suitor. Her desires needed to be purified so that she would desire none other than her Beloved. Her faith needed to be renewed. She had been waiting for her Bridegroom for so long that heartsickness had bowed her over and hopelessness had engulfed her soul. She needed an infusion of expectation in order to lift her eyes again.

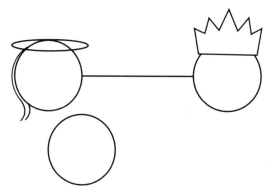

Figure 2

In Figure 2, a line has been drawn to connect the Bride and Bridegroom. That's because, in the words of John, "'He who has the bride is the bridegroom.'" Jesus has her. He owns her. He possesses her heart, her affections, her hopes, her desires, her aspirations, her loyalties. He holds her very heart in the palm of His hand. Her emotions may fluctuate from time to time, but when push comes to shove, there's really only One she loves. There's only One who has won her affections. There's only One to whom she is promised. He *has* her.

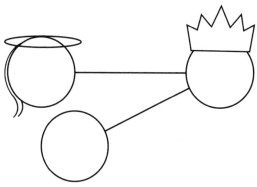

Figure 3

In Figure 3, notice that another line has been drawn, this time between the friend and the Bridegroom. That is because the friend is not called "the friend of the Bride," but rather "the friend of the Bridegroom."

It's important to emphasize that the friend's primary connection is to the Bridegroom, not the Bride. In this triad, the friend's loyalty is ultimately to the Bridegroom. The friend's primary concern is not to meet the Bride's expectations but to satisfy the Bridegroom's desires and needs.

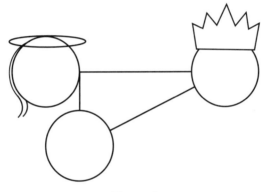

Figure 4

You'll notice that another line has been added, this time between the friend and the Bride. The line does not go directly to the Bride herself, however, but rather to the way she relates to the Bridegroom. I drew it this way to show that the friend isn't trying to build a connection with the Bride; rather, he's trying to grow her connection to the Groom. He has come alongside to strengthen and nurture the quality of her relationship with Jesus.

He reminds her of her Fiancé's beauty, grandeur, and splendor. The friend extols His kindness, gentleness, humility, wealth, prestige, personality, servanthood, understanding, wisdom, grace, mercy, power, and love. By the time the friend has finished talking about Him, the Bride's eyes are brimming with longing and eagerness for her Beloved.

The friend is willing to speak the truth to her in love. He's at liberty to speak the truth because he's not trying to impress her; rather, he's seeking to be faithful to her. So he doesn't only tell her the things she *wants* to hear, he tells her things she *needs* to hear.

You'll notice that the friend has a dual function in the parable. As regards his relationship to the Bridegroom, he is actually a part of the Bride. As regards his relationship to the Bride, he is the friend of the Bridegroom. In identity he's part of the Bride; in function he's a friend of the Bridegroom. So the appellation "friend of the Bridegroom" is a designation that points to his function as a minister to the Bride.

Bottom line, the friend serves the Bride out of allegiance to the Bridegroom. He and the Bridegroom have a strong history together, and the bond of affection that joins them makes the friend willing to go out of his way for the sake of the Bridegroom.

I want to illustrate that point from the life of Abraham. We'll come back to John the Baptist shortly, but for now, consider the example of Abraham as a friend of the Bridegroom God.

FIVE THINGS GOD ASKED OF ABRAHAM

The Bible records only five things that God asked of Abraham. The first one was, leave your hometown and go to an unspecified land (Genesis 12:1).

I don't think Abraham toiled long on that decision. The choice was to stay in Ur—I mean, whoop-di-do, dusty sandy Ur!—or go to a mystery land where he would inherit the whole country and bless the entire earth. He weighed the pros and cons and decided, "I'm out of here."

After he got to the promised land of Canaan, God made His second request: Walk the length and breadth of the land (Genesis 13:17). Abraham complied and took a long walk, east-to-west, north-to-south. It was a good land.

Request number three: "'Be blameless'" (Genesis 17:1). At this, I imagine Abraham having his first real pause. "Wait a minute," he's thinking, "You keep on changing the rules. You said if I left Ur that You'd give me this land, and that's what I signed up for. I was okay with taking a tour of the land, but now You're getting real personal. Blameless. Yikes. This is cramping my style. This affects how I live. Wow— You're asking me to be *blameless!*"

After pondering it for a while, I can suppose him concluding, "Well, He is, after all, giving me the whole land. I guess that gives Him the right to ask *something* of me. Okay, I'll devote my heart to walking blamelessly before Him. I mean, what more could He ask of a guy?"

But God *did* have something more to ask. Here came request number four: "Get circumcised" (see Genesis 17:10). I'm *positive* this request put Abraham on pause. "Waaaaaaaait a minute here! You're changing the rules again! Now You're getting *real* personal!"

Hello, guys. You see, to a guy, circumcision is personal. Extraordinarily so.

Amazingly, the Scripture tells us that Abraham got circumcised *that very day*, together with all the males in his household (Genesis 17:23). This is what God loved about Abraham: his implicit, immediate obedience.

"Wow, this is really intense!" I imagine him mulling. "This is the real deal. Here I am, 99 years old, and God is asking me to get circumcised. Well, okay. I'll do it. This is the ultimate sacrifice, and I'm willing to make it. For Him. I mean, what more could He ask of a guy?"

God had, however, one final request of Abraham.

Now it came to pass after these things that God tested Abraham, and said to him, "Abraham!" And he said, "Here I am." Then He said, "Take now your son, your only son Isaac, whom you love, and go to the land of Moriah, and offer him there as a burnt offering on one of the mountains of which I shall tell you" (Genesis 22:1-2).

Abraham was stunned. "God, this time You're not changing the rules; You're changing the *playing field*. Up to now Your requests have affected *my* life; but this one affects my *son's* life. You're blowing my theology to smithereens, God. You're asking me to commit *murder!* How could I possibly explain this to Sarah?"

This final request stopped Abraham cold. Abraham couldn't think of anything more personal than circumcision—until this. This was personal to the third power. This boy was the light of his eyes; this was his miracle child; this was his son of promise.

What was he to do? His mind was racing. What were his options? None, really. It was either obedience or...well, disobedience wasn't even an option. It was that raw, that stark. He had no alternative but to obey the voice and sacrifice his only son.

HOW ABRAHAM DEMONSTRATED HIS FRIENDSHIP WITH GOD

Abraham thought back to the time when God had offered him the world (see Romans 4:13). He had to admit that the dramatic breadth of God's offer did tug a little bit on his desires for wealth and significance. He could do the math. Accepting God's offer was, if nothing else, a smart business move. But now, this request to kill his son was removing every ounce of business from the equation. It was now 0% business and 100% personal.

The testimony of Scripture to Abraham's response is absolutely amazing.

> *So Abraham rose early in the morning and saddled his donkey, and took two of his young men with him, and Isaac his son; and he split the wood for the burnt offering, and arose and went to the place of which God had told him* (Genesis 22:3).

Immediate, radical obedience. Amazing!

Abraham went straight to the mountain, bound his son, placed him on the altar, and raised the knife. Abraham was fully intent on stabbing his son to death. But at that very moment he was stopped by the voice from heaven.

"'Abraham, Abraham!... Do not lay your hand on the lad, or do anything to him; for now I know that you fear God, since you have not withheld your son, your only son, from Me'" (Genesis 22:11-12).

Instead of sacrificing his son, Abraham was able to offer a ram that was caught in a nearby thicket.

The emotions of God toward Abraham on this occasion were so intense and passionate that when you read what follows, you get the impression God hardly knew how to contain Himself. God was so moved by Abraham's consecration and obedience that He opened the treasures of heaven and lavished upon Abraham the most extravagant promises imaginable.

> *Then the Angel of the LORD called to Abraham a second time out of heaven, and said: "By Myself I have sworn, says the LORD, because you have done this thing, and have not withheld your son, your only*

son—*blessing I will bless you, and multiplying I will multiply your descendants as the stars of the heaven and as the sand which is on the seashore; and your descendants shall possess the gate of their enemies. In your seed all the nations of the earth shall be blessed, because you have obeyed My voice"* (Genesis 22:15-18).

The Bible calls Abraham the "friend of God" (James 2:23). That friendship was sealed right here, at Moriah. When Abraham offered his son on that altar, he became a graphic illustration of God's plan of redemption.

"The day is coming, Abraham, when I will offer up My only Son, the Son I love, on a mountain. You don't have to drive the knife through your son's heart, but I do. There's a day coming when I will both take My Son to the mountain and kill Him. He will die for the sins of the world. Abraham, I needed someone who would show to the world what My plan of redemption is all about. I asked you to become that living example, and even though you didn't understand, you obeyed My voice and embodied that parable. Abraham, I didn't ask you to do this for *your* sake, I asked you to do it for *My* sake. *I'm* the One who needed this. You laid down your agenda in order to fulfill My agenda. Abraham, this is what friends are for. Friends lay their lives down for each other. Truly you are My friend! I'm *never* going to forget this."

By serving God's interests rather than his own, Abraham demonstrated what it means to be a true friend of the Bridegroom.

Now let's return to John the Baptist.

CHAPTER 3

PERSONAL
TO THE END

John served the Bridegroom for personal reasons—it had to do with friendship. But that attitude did not come naturally for John. It had to be forged in a crucible. Being a businessman came naturally; serving as a friend of the Bridegroom was a grace that had to be developed.

That's what John's wilderness was all about.

God sent John into the wilderness in order to prepare and shape him into a vessel that was fitting to be used for noble purposes.

You see, God was preparing to do something glorious in Israel. He was getting ready to send His Son to our planet. God was about to take up residence among men. The glory of it would be unprecedented. In order to prepare the people for the Messiah's advent, God had to raise up a forerunner.

John the Baptist was the man God picked to be that forerunner. To prepare and cultivate John's heart, God led him into the wilderness. During those long, lonely years in the wilderness, he fasted, prayed, and pored over the Scriptures. God sculpted his heart until he became a true friend of the Bridegroom.

In John the Baptist, God didn't need a powerful orator with business skills who would know how to build a ministry empire. God needed a friend. He needed someone who would do precisely what *He* wanted done, not what the *servant* wanted to do. To get that kind of friend, God had to make it personal for John.

Think, for a moment, about the power that must have rested on John's preaching and baptism ministry. He came at a time when God's people were hardened in unbelief; and yet, His preaching so moved the people that they came from all over to his baptism. If the numbers from the historian Josephus are accurate, John averaged upwards of 40,000 visitors per month.

The anointing on John's preaching was historic. The Holy Spirit power that rested on his words melted the most sin-hardened hearts. I call it a "repentance anointing." A similar kind of repentance anointing came upon Jonah, and as a result of his preaching the ungodly city of Nineveh repented en masse. The kind of anointing that was on Jonah was now resting on John's preaching. People were coming from all over, repenting of their sins, and getting baptized in water. The impact of his life was shaking the nation.

God knew it would take this level of anointing to shake the nation and prepare the way for Jesus. But who could be trusted with this kind of power, and then be able to process the diminishment redemptively when that anointing would begin to lift? An unusual vessel was needed, someone who would have zero business investment in the assignment. So when God chose John, He had to take John into the wilderness in order to make the thing personal.

The wilderness makes it personal.

If John were to have any kind of business aptitude working in him, the power of the anointing would become prostituted.

That is to say, John would be tempted to manipulate the anointing for personal advantage. God used the wilderness to knock the business thing out of John. When he was finally manifest to Israel, he was a true friend of God.

And when he was manifested, he roared onto the stage of an apostate nation.

MY MINISTRY CONSULTING BUSINESS

John's ministry was powerfully anointed, and it rocked the nation. Once a no-name wilderness hermit, he was suddenly catapulted onto the national scene as a force to be reckoned with. Crowds thronged to his meetings. God was visiting His people.

Now, I realize John had a powerful ministry. But if I had been alive at that time, I would have gladly offered him my services as a ministry consultant (I'm being tongue-in-cheek here). Had he asked, I would have offered him some suggestions for growing a stronger ministry. I know enough about church growth principles to know that John could have had an even greater ministry impact. Given the chance, I would have offered him these suggestions.

1. Relocate to a population center.

John, you have a good thing going here. There's authentic momentum in your meetings. You obviously have the favor of God on what you're doing because people are coming from all over. But you could take your ministry to a whole new level with just a few minor tweaks.

The first thing you need to change is your venue. You're stuck out here in "no man's land." People have to travel for days through dust basins to get to this God-forsaken wilderness. Just take what you're doing out here in Timbuktu and move it to a population center. John, you're getting amazing crowds for such a remote location; just think how many people would attend your meetings if you held them in a city! And if you'd like to know my recommendation, I propose Jerusalem. Establish a ministry center in Jerusalem and you'll not only shake the entire nation, you'll impact all the neighboring nations as well. By simply changing your location, you will unlock the international destiny and calling of God on your life.

2. Change your diet.

Bro, you gotta eat! John, you're a rack of bones. You fast a whole lot, and then when you do eat, it's locusts and wild honey. Baked locusts are simply too lean to adequately replenish your system. You're gaunt and pale. There's nothing appealing about your hollow cheeks and sunken eyes. To be honest, you actually look sort of spooky. People can't imitate your diet; it's just too rigorous. John, take it from me, it's time to put some meat on those bones. Simply get yourself up to a normal body weight and people will find it easier to receive from you.

3. Update your wardrobe.

John, what's with this Elijah motif you have going here? The camel hair and leather belt... It's not 90s, nor 80s, nor 70s; it's not even 60s. John, that look may have been in style 800 years ago, but it's seriously antiquated. It's not simply that you look outdated and irrelevant; you look austere, rough, and foreboding. You intimidate people simply with your presence. They stand aloof and listen to you from a distance. And who can blame them? You're skinny and you're scary.

And I have just one final piece of advice.

4. Stop insulting the people coming to your meetings.

John, many people are traveling for *days* to get here to hear you, and then once they get here, you insult them. These are the very people you're trying to build your ministry upon. To retain their commitment, you've got to stop calling them a "brood of vipers." I'm not saying you should butter them up with deceptive flattery; just stop insulting them.

Employ these four simple procedures, John, and I promise you, your ministry will go to the next level.

I can hear John's retort.

"You don't get it. I'm not trying to grow a ministry! I'm not in this thing to garner a larger following; I'm in this thing for a *Man*. You see, I had a heavenly encounter, and I was told by an angel that the Holy Spirit would descend upon a Man whom I would baptize. I was told that when I saw the Holy Spirit descend on Him, then I would know that He's the One who is to come. He's the Lamb of God who takes away the sins of the world. I do everything I do for a Man. It's personal for me."

Ministry was a personal matter for John, not a venture to be capitalized upon for maximum impact. His example is arresting to us who live in an age when many ministers are using shrewd business principles to gather larger crowds. Many of today's conferences for pastors and leaders reinforce that approach to ministry by focusing on how pastors can grow their churches from 100 to 200 people. The felt need of many leaders in our generation is how to break through their current growth barrier into the next level of attendance. Where are the voices calling us back to the authenticity that John demonstrated—the authenticity of looking with longing for the advent of one's true Friend?

A RUB BETWEEN TWO MINISTRIES

While the ministry wasn't business for John, his disciples were in a different place. For them, actually, it *was* business.

We get a feel for their perspective in an incident recorded in John 3. There was a brief window of time, prior to John's imprisonment, in which both John and Jesus were ministering simultaneously but in different locations. Two separate revival crusades being convened at the same time gave opportunity for carnal comparisons. The Jewish leaders, who actually had a problem with both revival meetings, were the first to compare the two. They came to John's disciples with a message they hoped would pit John against Jesus.

"Are you aware," the Jewish leaders most likely asked John's disciples, "that the guy John baptized and publicly endorsed—Jesus of Nazareth—is holding His own revival meetings? What's more, His disciples are baptizing people now too. Some people are saying you no longer need John's baptism, you just need Jesus' baptism. When you listen to the message and see how the people are being baptized, it makes you feel like somebody is copying somebody. They're a replica of John's meetings. With one major difference: Jesus' meetings have a whole lot more people at them than John ever had."

"Haven't you noticed," the Jewish leaders continued, "that John's meetings are declining in attendance? The reason is simple. The crowds are siphoning over to Jesus' meetings. The word on the street is that John's meetings are outdated. Old school. I bet your master didn't realize that, in endorsing Jesus of Nazareth, he was spelling the demise of his own ministry."

This update from the Jews alarmed John's disciples.

They took it straight to their master.

> *And they came to John and said to him, "Rabbi, He*
> *who was with you beyond the Jordan, to whom you*
> *have testified—behold, He is baptizing, and all are*
> *coming to Him!"* (John 3:26).

They were distressed by the plummeting attendance at John's meetings, and likely expected him to share their concern. The entire team had come to depend upon the gifts and donations of the people, and this new development no doubt explained why both attendance and offerings had taken a hit. John's disciples probably kept the books and so were painfully aware that the business side of the ministry was in a tight place. What would John have to say about Jesus and His growing popularity? Here's John's remarkable answer.

John answered and said, "A man can receive nothing unless it has been given to him from heaven. You yourselves bear me witness, that I said, 'I am not the Christ,' but, 'I have been sent before Him.' He who has the bride is the bridegroom; but the friend of the bridegroom, who stands and hears him, rejoices greatly because of the bridegroom's voice. Therefore this joy of mine is fulfilled. He must increase, but I must decrease" (John 3:27-30).

John was basically saying to his disciples, "My popularity and the impact of my meetings are waning, and I've got more joy than ever. The One for whom I have watched and waited has finally come, so my joy is complete. He must increase, but I must continue to decrease."

John's disciples were concerned about falling numbers, but John was undisturbed by that because of his joy over hearing the Bridegroom's voice. For John, it was all about a Man. It was personal.

WHEN THE BRIDE FORGETS YOUR NAME

When the Bridegroom showed up, the Bride forsook the friend (John the Baptist) and followed after the Bridegroom. In a human or natural sense, it would have seemed understandable if John had been a little upset with Jesus over that.

"I've been wearing camel hair for You. I've been eating locusts for You. I served Your Bride at a time when she wasn't even sure she wanted You, but I turned her heart toward You. And now that You're finally here, what's my thanks? You haven't invited me to speak at even one of Your meetings. Now that You've showed up, the Bride has totally forgotten about me and she has gone chasing after You. I'm not feeling very appreciated right now."

But no, that wasn't John's attitude. His attitude was more like, "She has forgotten my name, and I couldn't be happier. Because the Bridegroom is here."

The true friends of the Bridegroom who serve the Bride know there will come a day when she will forget their name. When Jesus returns to earth, she will totally forget the friend for the joy of being in the Bridegroom's embrace. I imagine the Bride scratching her head and saying, "I remember being told once by Mr. Whatcha-Ma-Call-It...Oh my, I think his name was Pastor...um, Pastor...uh, Pastor... Oh, forget it. Jesus, I can't even remember his name. But it's okay because You're here with me now!"

In that moment, when the Bride isn't giving him even the slightest thought, the true friend says, "She has totally forgotten who I am, and now my joy is complete!"

For John, it was personal all the way to the end.

CHAPTER 4

NAVIGATING DIMINISHMENT

W hen Jesus showed up, the Bride was so taken with the Bridegroom that she began to forget about John the Baptist. She forgot how faithfully and selflessly he had served her. It was essential that Jesus increase in her eyes, and in order for that to happen properly, John had to decrease. "'He must increase, but I must decrease'" (John 3:30).

John knew that it was his destiny to decrease. He was given divine information about that in advance, so when the diminishment began to happen he was able to cooperate with it redemptively. But that didn't mean it was either easy or enjoyable.

Even though he knew diminishment was coming, John the Baptist didn't really know how to prepare for it because he didn't know what shape it would take. Diminishment usually comes in packages we didn't anticipate. In John's case, it took the unexpected form of imprisonment. Prison became so distressful to his soul that he almost became offended at Jesus for not delivering him from it (see Matthew 11:6). The thing that saved him from being offended was his personal loyalty to Jesus. If it had been business, John would have become a casualty.

Diminishment can be terribly challenging to navigate gracefully. And yet it's one of the most commonly experienced dynamics of our human sojourn.

Virtually all of us experience alternating periods of both increase and diminishment throughout life. Like the tides of the sea, we'll have a season in which increase seems to flow to us, only to be followed by an ebbing tide of decrease. Diminishment is an essential ingredient in the cycles of healthy living because unbroken success is detrimental to character formation.

Diminishment is a necessary follow-up to success because without it we won't process the success in a healthy way.

There's something dizzying about "the meth of momentum." It can go to your head. We see its effect, for example, in the life of Joshua. After crossing the Jordan on dry ground and then watching the walls of Jericho collapse at his feet, Joshua was feeling the rush of what I call "ministry momentum." As a result, he didn't consult God about the battle of Ai. He suffered a defeat at Ai because he was feeling so confident in his stride. After finally conquering Ai, once again he lacked the presence of mind to consult God about the ambassadors from Gibeon. He made two serious errors in judgment because, while caught up in the wave of success, he lost track of his need to consult God.

God found it necessary to discipline Joshua, so that he would learn to steward success in maturity. What form did that discipline take? In one word, diminishment. God used diminishment to restore Joshua to meekness.

Meekness is the fruit of a proper response to diminishment.

We see this in the life of Moses. When Moses went from the 40-year glory of the Egyptian palace to the 40-year diminishment of the Midianite wilderness, it prepared him in meekness for one of the greatest entrustments of leadership ever given by God to a man. Consider how great Moses' meekness was. When God offered to wipe out the nation of Israel and start all over again with Moses as the sole father of the nation, Moses was able to decline the intoxicating offer (see Exodus 32:9-14). Had Korah been granted the same offer he would have said, "Let it be done to me according to Your word." But Moses responded in meekness because of character formed in the crucible of the wilderness.

JACOB KNEW HOW TO DICKER

Jacob was another man with whom God used diminishment in order to produce meekness.

Jacob was a tough guy who definitely had a hankering for business. He swindled the birthright and blessing from his brother, Esau. Later, he managed to get the greater share of Laban's flocks and herds. He was a "wheeler-dealer." He was shrewd and savvy. Making money came naturally.

God didn't need Jacob to be a father, however, who could impart his business skills to Joseph. He needed Jacob to be a father who could impart the passion of a personal walk with God from a heart of meekness.

That's what Peniel was all about. It was at Peniel that God appeared to him and wrestled with him all night (Genesis 32:24-31). By taking his hip out (an intense form of diminishment), God dealt a death blow to that business spirit in Jacob and replaced it with a heart of meekness. By changing his name from Jacob to Israel, God got personal. When God maimed Jacob and changed his name, it made his walk with God intensely personal.

Jacob was a man who had used his strength all his life to push forward to his desired goals. He was a pusher—until his hip got taken out, that is. When Jacob's hip took the hit and he became a limping man, he lost his power to push. God broke Jacob's strength in order to produce meekness in his soul. In turn, it was the strength of meekness formed in Jacob that enabled him to rear a young forerunner named Joseph. Without Jacob's diminishment, it's unlikely we would have had our Joseph.

A Jacob generation has to be reduced to a limp before it can raise up a Joseph generation.

DIMINISHMENT MADE IT PERSONAL

Jacob actually experienced several seasons of diminishment throughout his lifetime. By the time Jacob had finished the roller-coaster ride, his walk with God had become vibrantly personal.

It's the seasons of diminishment that make things personal.

To see how this happened with Jacob, our focus turns to the latter years of his life. Jacob's last 17 years ended in prosperity and blessing, but immediately prior to that grand finale he had 22 grueling years of diminishment and spiritual barrenness. We know nothing about those 22 long years in Jacob's life because the Genesis narrative is entirely preoccupied with telling us Joseph's story.

It was 22 years from the time Joseph was taken away from his father to the time he was restored to his father.

During those long, silent years, Jacob must have wondered, "God, what is going on between You and me? What are You thinking about when You look at me? Why are my years consumed with ceaseless sorrow?"

At the end of those 22 years, just before his deliverance, Jacob entered the greatest crisis of his life. His household was in the grip of a horrible famine, his son Simeon was just recently imprisoned in Egypt, and the man who imprisoned him now wanted Benjamin. He had lost Joseph and Simeon, and was about to lose Benjamin—not to mention that he was losing his ability to provide for his household in the midst of the severe famine. Even God seemed to be against him.

We know how the story ended, though. Jacob got back all his sons, and he was transported to Egypt where his household had ample provisions during the famine. Jacob lived out the final 17 years of his life in honor and blessing.

When God reversed Jacob's fortunes and established him in prosperity, Jacob took it personally. We know that because of how he expressed himself. At the end of his life, while addressing his sons, he made a stunning statement to them. That stunning statement is found in the following quote.

> *"Joseph is a fruitful bough, a fruitful bough by a well; his branches run over the wall. The archers have bitterly grieved him, shot at him and hated him. But his bow remained in strength, and the arms of <u>his hands were made strong by the hands of the Mighty God of Jacob</u> (from there is the Shepherd, the Stone of Israel), by the God of your father who will help you, and by the Almighty who will bless you with blessings of heaven above, blessings of the deep that lies beneath, blessings of the breasts and of the womb"* (Genesis 49:22-25).

The stunning statement I want you to notice is underlined above: "his hands were made strong by the hands of the Mighty God of Jacob."

This is Jacob calling God "the mighty God of Jacob." That would be like me saying to my children, "Let me tell you about the mighty God of Bob."

Jacob was saying, "He's *my* God. He has shown me that our relationship is personal to Him. I knew it was personal when He restored Joseph to me. Now I know that I am His and He is mine."

I want what Jacob touched. I want it to be so personal that I can commend my children to "the God of Bob."

CHAPTER 5

HIRELINGS AND
MERCHANDISERS

All of us want to believe we serve Jesus for personal reasons, and yet it's so easy for us to slip over into a mode of marketing the ministry to which we're called. We convince ourselves we're promoting our ministry only for the glory of God, and yet the lines of our motivations start to become blurry. Those who approach the work of the ministry with a business mentality hazard succumbing to a hireling spirit.

> *"But a hireling, he who is not the shepherd, one who does not own the sheep, sees the wolf coming and leaves the sheep and flees; and the wolf catches the sheep and scatters them. The hireling flees because he is a hireling and does not care about the sheep"* (John 10:12-13).

A hireling is someone who tends the flock because he's in it for the money. It's a job. He's hired for a specific task and gets paid appropriately for his time and labors.

For the shepherd, however, the flock is a personal matter. His entire life is wrapped up in the welfare of the flock. Any harm done to the flock impacts him directly.

Here's a question worth asking: Am I a hireling, or am I a shepherd? Do I serve the flock of Christ because I get a paycheck, or because the welfare of the flock is everything I live for?

One way you can tell is by evaluating your response when a predator assaults the flock. A shepherd stays near the flock until the danger is past; a hireling withdraws.

It was when the flock was under attack that David's true heart as a shepherd was manifest. One day a lion came to devour one of the sheep (1 Samuel 17:34-36). David was probably thinking, "That's my father's lamb you have in your mouth! Over my dead body will you have that lamb!" David pulled the lamb from the lion's mouth; then he took the lion by its beard and killed it. He literally took his life in his hands to save a sheep.

A hireling would have never done such a thing. He would have replied, "They don't pay me to do lions." A hireling would have allowed the lion to take the lamb and then would have told the shepherd, "Before I could do anything, the lion had escaped with the lamb." Mentally, however, he would be thinking, "You're going to have to pay me a whole lot more if you want me to take on lions!"

There is a hireling spirit in the church today. It is a spirit that looks at an area of need and says, "That's not my job. I'm not paid to do that." It's a spirit that says, "If they want me to do that, they're going to have to pay me." It's a spirit that says, "You can have me if you're willing to pay more than the other church." In other words, it's not personal, it's business.

TURNING MINISTRY INTO BUSINESS

The Bible gives us warnings from the lives of several people who suffered great loss because they allowed a business mentality to infiltrate their obedience to God.

Gehazi (2 Kings 5). Gehazi was Elisha's servant who saw an opportunity to enrich himself as a consequence of Naaman's healing. Because of his greed, the leprosy from which Naaman was healed came upon Gehazi, and he was a leper till the day of his death.

Ananias and Sapphira (Acts 5). Ananias and Sapphira never broke free from their love of money, and in the end that allegiance was stronger than their personal loyalty to Christ. They tried to use their material assets to gain favor with the apostles and the church, and the Holy Spirit killed them as a sign to the church.

Judas Iscariot (John 12:4-8). Judas Iscariot had heard Jesus teach, "'You cannot serve God and mammon'" (Matthew 6:24), but for some reason that message never penetrated his heart. Being with Jesus never did become personal for him. It was all business, right from the get-go. Judas was on a quest for personal advancement. Consequently, he struggled for three years to give his heart in personal allegiance to Jesus. By continuing to honor the god of money (he would steal from Jesus' treasury, John 12:6), eventually that business bent consumed him and dragged him to his destruction (Acts 1:18).

Balaam (Numbers 22-24). Balaam wanted to curse Israel because he knew Balak would give him a fat honorarium for doing so. God resisted Balaam, however, and would only let him bless Israel. In the end, just like any good businessman, Balaam still found a way to get remunerated. He told Balak that although he couldn't curse Israel, there was a way Israel could bring a curse upon themselves. All Balak had to do, according to Balaam, was send his young women to the Israelite camp to seduce and lure the Israelites into sexual immorality (see Revelation 2:14). Balaam knew that fornication would cause the Israelites to incur the curse he himself could not pronounce upon them. Balak compensated Balaam handsomely for the advice.

Micah spoke of prophets who ministered primarily for remuneration:

> *Thus says the LORD concerning the prophets who make my people stray; who chant "Peace" while they chew with their teeth, but who prepare war against him who puts nothing into their mouths... Her heads judge for a bribe, her priests teach for pay, and her prophets divine for money. Yet they lean on the LORD, and say, "Is not the LORD among us? No harm can come upon us"* (Micah 3:5,11)

For the Pharisees in Jesus' day, the work of the ministry had largely become about ministry profile, name recognition, human honor, money, and self-preservation. Jesus warned His disciples about the leaven of the Pharisees because He knew that all of us have the potential to fall into the same trap.

JESUS DRIVES OUT THE BUSINESSMEN

A hireling spirit had overtaken the temple in Jesus' day. Merchants had set up shop on the temple grounds. Business was brisk.

It's John who tells us how Jesus visited His Father's house of prayer with a whip in hand.

> *Now the Passover of the Jews was at hand, and Jesus went up to Jerusalem. And He found in the temple those who sold oxen and sheep and doves, and the money changers doing business. When He had made a whip of cords, He drove them all out of the*

> temple, with the sheep and the oxen, and poured out
> the changers' money and overturned the tables. And
> He said to those who sold doves, "Take these things
> away! Do not make My Father's house a house of
> merchandise!" Then His disciples remembered that it
> was written, "Zeal for Your house has eaten Me up"
> (John 2:13-17).

Jesus cleansed the house of prayer a second time, at the
end of His earthly ministry. No whip is mentioned the second time, but the same violent zeal is demonstrated. Here's
Mark's account.

> So they came to Jerusalem. Then Jesus went into the
> temple and began to drive out those who bought and
> sold in the temple, and overturned the tables of the
> money changers and the seats of those who sold doves.
> And He would not allow anyone to carry wares
> through the temple. Then He taught, saying to them,
> "Is it not written, 'My house shall be called a house of
> prayer for all nations'? But you have made it a 'den of
> thieves'" (Mark 11:15-17).

Here's what was going on. Many of those coming to
Jerusalem during a festival traveled long distances, and it
was burdensome to bring with them animals to sacrifice.
The Lord provided them with an alternative. They could
sell their lamb back home, bring the proceeds with them,
and purchase a lamb in Jerusalem to offer to the Lord. Thus,
many worshipers arrived at Jerusalem eager to buy a lamb or
a couple doves with the money they had brought.

Waiting for them was another eager group: those who
sold doves and sacrificial animals. Travelers with currency
from other nations first had to exchange their funds with
the money changers for local currency. Exchange rates were

at premium levels during festivals. Then the pilgrims had little recourse but to purchase lambs and doves at the going rates in Jerusalem. Those who sold doves had agreed on a pricing system that assured them of generous profits, and pilgrims either paid the inflated price or had no sacrifice to offer. The local merchants were taking advantage of the vulnerability of those visiting Jerusalem and earning much of their annual salary in one fell swoop.

It was because of the inflated profits the merchants were able to earn during festivals that Jesus called the whole operation a "'den of thieves.'" And it was all happening right inside the temple courts!

A fire blazed in Jesus' eyes as He overthrew the tables of the money changers and the seats of those who sold doves. Everyone saw something in the sternness of His countenance that caused them to cower in trepidation. In the heat of the moment, I can imagine the merchants wanting to saying something like, "Whoa, aren't we being a bit intense? Cool Your jets, Lord. I mean, aren't You over-reacting just a little bit? You're acting as though this is personal. There's nothing personal going on here, Lord, it's totally business." To that kind comment I can imagine Jesus' rejoinder, "When you take advantage of My Bride and exploit her vulnerability, it's not business to Me, it's personal."

WE WILL BE JUDGED INDIVIDUALLY

The merchants saw a fire in Jesus' eyes when He cleansed the temple. And there's a Day coming when you and I will look into those same fiery eyes. We would do well to prepare for that appointment.

Your appearance before Christ on the Day of Judgment is going to be a very personal encounter between you and Jesus. When your eyes lock with His, the only important thing in the universe at that moment will be the words that come out of His mouth. The big question is, will He claim to have a personal relationship with you?

> *"Not everyone who says to Me, 'Lord, Lord,' shall enter the kingdom of heaven, but he who does the will of My Father in heaven. Many will say to Me in that day, 'Lord, Lord, have we not prophesied in Your name, cast out demons in Your name, and done many wonders in Your name?' And then I will declare to them, 'I never knew you; depart from Me, you who practice lawlessness!'"* (Matthew 7:21-23).

In that day, it really doesn't matter how personal you thought your connection with Christ was. You can say, "Lord, Lord," but the great issue will not be whether it seemed personal to *you*; the great issue will be, was it personal for *Him*? Did *He* know you? Was your proximity to Him near enough so that He *could* know you?

If you were in it for business, the Day will make it very clear.

When Jesus spoke of how He will judge the nations at his return, He used very personal language. To the saints He will say, "Inasmuch as you did it to one of the least of these My brethren, you did it to Me'" (Matthew 25:40). In other words, Jesus will say to the righteous, "When you served My brethren, I took it personally."

And to the wicked He will say, "When you didn't serve one of the least of these, I took it personally. It was *Me* you neglected" (paraphrase of Matthew 25:45).

Are you ready for a profoundly personal, individual, face-to-face meeting with Jesus? The appointment is already on His calendar.

CHAPTER 6

SCORING
WITH THE BRIDE

O ne of the things Jesus will judge, in the last day, will be how His friends handled themselves around His Bride. This is real important to Jesus, even now. He's wondering, "Are you serving her in a way that helps *Me*, or helps *you*?"

One of the most searching questions He's ever asked me is this: "After she's spent an evening with you, does My Bride come away from the meeting talking about you or Me?"

I'm the first to admit I've tried to score points with the Bride. My soul has a propensity to revel in her accolades and approbation. If I allow myself to feed off her praises, then I find myself adjusting my conduct around her in order to get more of the same. Now, instead of telling her what she *needs* to hear, I'm telling her what she *wants* to hear.

It's impossible to be a prophetic voice to the Bride while at the same time seeking her approval and appreciation.

PREACHING CHRIST BUT PROCLAIMING YOURSELF

Paul once said, "For we do not preach ourselves, but Christ" (2 Corinthians 4:5). I've discovered it's possible to preach Christ and proclaim yourself. What I mean is, it's possible to use all the right words—"It's only for Your glory, Lord!"—talk about Jesus, and speak things that are theologically sound and accurate, but conduct yourself in a way that draws attention to yourself. If you present your message in a certain way, the Bride will be impressed with your brainpower, with your mastery of language, with the coherence of your thought processes, with the effectiveness of your communication skills, and with your ability to present a message that leaves everyone awestruck. She leaves the meeting saying, "That sermon was a masterpiece!"

It's possible to sing about Jesus and proclaim yourself. Your song has all the right words in it and points to Jesus the whole way through, but by the time you're finished singing it, the Bride is talking about *you*. "What a voice! And what an anointing! Her passion comes through so effectively! Great song selection too, I loved the jazzy feel of the song. I hope she puts that song on a CD."

I've prayed many times, "Lord Jesus, have mercy on me, and deliver me from this tendency to present myself in such a way that the Bride takes notice of me and my service to her. After I've spent an evening with Your Bride, I don't want *my* name to be the name on her lips. I want her to be talking about *You!* Help me, Lord Jesus, to be a loyal friend to You!"

A loyal friend is always careful never to seek from the Bride that which is the Bridegroom's domain (the affections and veneration of the Bride).

THE DIVINE ROMANCE

Jesus has commissioned His friends to serve His Bride until He comes for the wedding. It's the friend's job to serve her needs, to equip and prepare her for her wedding day, and to help her guard her heart until the Bridegroom returns. The friend represents God's appointed leaders in the body of Christ and their ministry role to the Bride.

Now, there's a certain chemistry between Jesus and His Bride. Their relationship is not even remotely sexual in nature, but it certainly is affectionate and passionate. Call it magnetism; call it electricity; call it sparks; call it chemistry. Whatever the right word for it, the Bride definitely has a "thing" for the Bridegroom, and vice versa. They're both smitten!

It's a dynamic that doesn't exist between Jesus and the angels. The angels love the Son of God, but not with the same romantic intimacy. They don't partake of the Bride's longing, nor are they the recipients of the Bridegrooms yearning desires. The angels look at it and are mystified. One angel asks another, "What's the deal with the Bride and the Bridegroom? I mean, what does He see in her?"

The other angel replies, "I know what you mean. I don't get it either. Is it just me, or is the whole thing irrational?"

"I'm not sure," the first angel replies. "Let's ask Gabriel, maybe he knows something we don't."

So the two go to Gabriel and ask, "Gabriel, can you help us understand the allure between the Bridegroom and the Bride? What's the attraction? Why is Jesus so enchanted with her?"

"Beats me," replies Gabriel. "I'm as clueless as you. But my hunch is that the magnetism pulling them together is stronger than we even realize."

As friends of the Bridegroom, here's what pastors and worship leaders and teachers and home group leaders do: They enter the force field that exists between the Bride and Bridegroom and seek to serve it. They try to fan the flames of love. The Bride is an immature lover, and she needs help and coaching to discover how to give her heart in abandoned obedience to her Lord. As the friend exhorts her, she slowly learns how to give her heart more perfectly to her Beloved.

The friend steps into the love relationship that the King of the universe has with His Bride and seeks to help it along. What nerve! Talk about frightening!

THE BRIDE NOTICES THE FRIEND

When you're especially skillful at facilitating the love exchange, the Bride notices. She turns to the friend and says, "Wow, you're good! You're really skillful at representing the Bridegroom. I like it when you lead."

When the Bride begins to shower you with attention, it's heady and exhilarating. She is extremely attractive, and she's got a whole lot of love to give. Usually she is directing her affections to her Bridegroom; but when she turns and notices the friend, it can be downright intoxicating.

"We just love this church, Pastor!" she gushes. "We're not going to say anything about the church we left, but suffice it to say, since coming to your church it's like we're coming up out of a long, dark grave. The way you break open the word, Pastor, it's so easy to understand and so relevant to our lives. Even our kids enjoy going to church now. They get upset when we have to miss! Coming to this church is the best thing that ever happened to us. For the first time in our lives, we feel like we actually have a Pastor. Thank you for just being *you!*"

The Bride also has her way of affirming worship leaders.

"I just love that new song you wrote!" she enthuses. "It really expresses what the Spirit is saying to the church right now. And I love the chord changes too. I'm grateful to God for the others who lead worship at our church, but my heart always leaps inside when I see it's your turn to lead. I wouldn't say this to anyone else, but you really are our favorite worship leader."

There really is no area of service or leadership that is

exempt from the effusive praises of the Bride.

"I'm so grateful for your ministry to the youth of this church," she says to the youth leader. "We were really concerned about the spiritual welfare of our two teenagers and were crying out to God for an answer. Then, when He led them to your youth group, it was an answer from heaven. Now they're on fire for God, and it's because of the anointing on your life and the way you care. I'm not sure the Pastor even knows this, but you're the reason we're at this church now!"

The Bride is inevitably going to lavish her attention on the Bridegroom's friend. It's unavoidable. She's not trying to score with the friend; she's just being grateful. But when it happens, the Bridegroom is watching intently to see how His friend handles it. What happens inside His friend's heart when the Bride turns her affections toward him? Will he begin to flirt with the Bride?

A HYPERACTIVE TROUBADOUR

The friend of the Bridegroom is like a troubadour. We're troubadours—facilitators of love. We serve the love relationship between Jesus and His Bride so that it might grow and come into full maturity and complete fulfillment.

A troubadour, by definition, is a musician and/or singer who uses his craft to infuse vocabulary and passion into the language of love. He facilitates love with his lyrics and melodies.

The following scenario is almost too absurd to imagine. But imagine taking your girlfriend to a restaurant for a romantic meal together. You're trying to win her heart. You're delightedly surprised, after being seated, to discover that the restaurant has hired an acoustic jazz guitarist for the evening to play romantic music for the dining couples. "This is perfect," you think to yourself. "Live music. Can't get more romantic than this. She's going to melt!"

The troubadour notices you and your beautiful date, and he slowly makes his way toward your table. You're thinking, "Excellent! Personalized love songs." As he plays, you lock eyes with your sweetheart, your voices become soft, and your hearts grow tender.

Then the troubadour takes one step too close. The guitar is no longer a background effect; it's now front and center. His singing is getting louder than you would like. You ask your girlfriend to repeat what she just said because the music was a bit too loud.

But the music comes even closer, and even louder. Now, instead of feeling like the music is helping you romance your date, you feel like it's distracting your ability to enjoy each other. Your girlfriend is trying to track with your conversation, but she can't help but glance over at the troubadour.

When the troubadour catches her eye, he takes another step closer. Now he's actually touching your table! He has turned now and isn't singing to the two of you any longer; he's singing only to your girl. She glances your way, but when she does he hits a chord extra hard on the guitar, and her eyes jerk back to the troubadour.

You're sitting there and thinking, "This guy is hitting on my girlfriend, in my presence, right in the middle of our night out!"

The troubadour has become a rival.

It seems preposterous to us to imagine a troubadour hitting on a girl in the presence of her guy. But many of us do it. We call ourselves the friend of the Bridegroom, but then we begin to court the attentions of the Bride in the presence of the Bridegroom Himself!

When the friend of the Groom starts to flirt with the Bride, he's no longer a friend to the Bridegroom—he's a competitor.

CHAPTER 7

SPIRITUAL
EUNUCHS

The last thing we want is to become competitors of Jesus. And Jesus has similar feelings. The last thing Jesus wants is for His friends to enter into an adversarial role with Him because they've conducted themselves inappropriately in the presence of His Bride.

Jesus is willing to do whatever it takes to preserve the integrity of His friends, so that they don't try to establish their own personal relationship with the Bride. In order to help His friends preserve their integrity with the Bride, Jesus will make eunuchs of His friends. He will make us into spiritual eunuchs so that we might serve the Bride as His true friends.

I want to explain what I mean by "spiritual eunuchs," and to do that I need to show how eunuchs were used by royalty in ancient times.

THE ROLE OF EUNUCHS

The book of Acts tells a fascinating story about a man who served the queen of Ethiopia as a eunuch in her court. He was traveling back to Ethiopia from a pilgrimage to

Jerusalem, and could not understand his readings in Isaiah about the Messiah. To help him understand, the Spirit of God sent Philip so that Philip could show him how Jesus fulfilled the prophecies of Isaiah.

We are told that this man was "a eunuch of great authority under Candace the queen of the Ethiopians, who had charge of all her treasury" (Acts 8:27). So we find ourselves asking the question, "Why would a queen place a *eunuch* over all her treasury?"

The answer would be found in analyzing the nature of the relationship between the queen and her treasurer. The queen would need someone who is brilliant and competent to serve as her national treasurer, and she would need to interface with that person in some very personal and private ways. Assuming that Candace had a husband, I can imagine her husband piping up at this point, "Whoever works with you as your chief treasurer, he'll be working very closely with you, and I need to be assured he won't try anything inappropriate around you. Whoever you choose, therefore, must be a eunuch."

So in the case of Candace, she used eunuchs in primary roles of leadership in her court, knowing that they would not interfere in her relationship with her husband.

Eunuchs were used not only by queens, but also by kings. It was common practice in ancient times for a king to forcibly make eunuchs of men and then bring them into his court as servants. It appears, for example, that this is what Nebuchadnezzar did with Daniel and his three friends, Shadrach, Meshach, and Abed-nego (Daniel 1:7). "Why would a king," you might ask, "want eunuchs in his court?" For basically the same reason Candace had eunuchs around her. A king would have eunuchs in his court because of his bride. Once made eunuchs, these men could be trusted in the presence of the queen.

Kings of old often had their choice of the most desirable maidens in the land. The bride chosen by the king would be stunningly beautiful, which was a plus for the king. But there was one negative facet to her beauty: Who could he trust in her presence? If given the opportunity, would a prince in his kingdom try to cozy up to her? The king was choosy, therefore, about those to whom he would entrust the care of his bride. Not everybody could be trusted with an All-Access Pass.

The solution was simply this: Entrust her to the care of eunuchs. They're strong, protective, capable, and smart. And they're safe. They're safe company for the bride.

Why was a eunuch safe company for the bride? Because a eunuch had cut away from his life the mechanism that would cause him to desire the bride for himself.[1]

---

1   On one occasion, after I had spoken on spiritual eunuchs at a meeting, one of the leaders said to me afterwards, "That's not circumcision, that's castration!"

In contemplating the ramifications of castration, I am reminded about something my friend, Jeff Ell, brought to my attention during one of our visits together. He said to me, "I am aware of only one animal that is used in the New Testament to point in any kind of symbolic way to the nature of a New Testament minister." He then mentioned the ox, which is cited in 1 Corinthians 9:9 and 1 Timothy 5:18, where Paul quotes the Old Testament, "'You shall not muzzle an ox while it treads out the grain.'"

Jeff asked me, "Do you know what an ox is?" I told him I guessed it was a unique breed of cattle. But I was wrong.

An ox is not a distinct species from the cow (genus *Bos*), but the same general species. An ox is simply an old, castrated bull. In its youth, a castrated bull is called a steer; when it's over three years old, it's called an ox.

A bull can be a dangerous animal. Not only is a bull heavy and strong, it is often temperamental and ornery, easily irritated, highly territorial, and quite lethal (Psalm 22:12).

A bull is useful for sport by rodeo riders because of its independent, surly nature. You're not going to train a bull, however, and connect it to a yoke. If you want a bull to be useful for agricultural work, you're going to have to castrate it.

Once castrated and matured, an ox is a highly valuable asset for a farmer. Oxen are strong, hard-working, teachable, docile, and able to endure

A eunuch was free to serve the bride without wanting her or anything she could offer.

A eunuch received everything he needed from the king. The king provided him with food, drink, clothing, lodging, and a salary. The bride couldn't give him anything he didn't already have. So a eunuch wasn't trying to get anything from the bride. He was able to serve her in total freedom without needing or seeking anything in return.

A EUNUCH NAMED HEGAI

The nature of the relationship between the bride and a eunuch is exemplified in this verse from the book of Esther:

> *Now when the turn came for Esther the daughter of Abihail the uncle of Mordecai, who had taken her as his daughter, to go in to the king, she requested nothing but what Hegai the king's eunuch, the custodian of the women, advised* (Esther 2:15).

Ahasuerus, king of Persia, had appointed Hegai, the

---

long hours of labor each day.

Oxen are not so commonplace on American farms anymore. Their role has been supplanted by power equipment. But I remember seeing quite a few oxen in the fields when I visited Vietnam. In some nations of the earth, oxen are still used to plow the soil and pull heavy loads.

The church is called "God's field" (1 Corinthians 3:9). Even as a farmer uses oxen to prepare his field for harvest, God prepares His harvest by using servants whose strengths have been tamed and trained that they might accomplish much for the Kingdom of God.

How fascinating that God would characterize His New Covenant leaders as *oxen!* Something in them has been cut away, making them useful for service to the Master.

I find it equally fascinating that when Ezekiel had his vision of the four living creatures who surround God's throne, he said each one had four faces. They each had the face of a man, a lion, an eagle, and an ox (Ezekiel 1:10). That they had the face of an ox speaks of incredible strength brought under the power of meekness in order to be useful as a servant to the Almighty.

eunuch, to serve his bride. He knew he could trust Hegai to serve Esther faithfully without violating her in any way.

This meant that Hegai qualified to serve Esther in a most intimate and personal way. He might give her a manicure or pedicure. He might toss and run his hands through her hair as he experimented with finding the right hairdo. He might give her a facial. He might help fit her dress. He might lather her with lotions and dabble her with just the right fragrance. Whatever Hegai's role in Esther's preparation might have been, he was able to execute it judiciously without fantasizing or touching her inappropriately.

In this living allegory, Ahasuerus represents the High King of heaven. Esther represents the Bride of Christ. And Hegai represents leaders in the body of Christ who have been made spiritual eunuchs for the sake of preparing the Bride.

A EUNUCH IS SAFE COMPANY FOR THE BRIDE

The great King of glory is getting ready to marry a most beautiful Bride. Right now she is in preparation, receiving beauty treatments and being made ready for the King. To get her ready, the King is choosing eunuchs to serve her. These eunuchs are leaders in the body of Christ who have had severed from their lives the mechanisms within their souls that would cause them to want the Bride's affections for themselves.

How does God make spiritual eunuchs? He redemptively uses the biting blade of difficult circumstances to do such a deep surgical work in the life of His servants that the very motives and matters of their hearts are profoundly transformed. By the time the knife has finished its work, the servant seeks only the honor of God (John 5:44).

Then, when the Bride lavishes her attention on a

eunuch-leader, it has no power over the eunuch. Her praises have no more effect on the heart of a eunuch-leader than a magnet has power over a piece of fruit. There is no metallic substance within the heart of a eunuch-leader which the magnetism of her attentions can find.

If, however, the King has a leader who has not come under the knife, when the Bride's magnetic attentions are turned on him or her something inside that leader is drawn toward the Bride. When a leader enjoys and feeds off the Bride's honor, something inside that leader reaches out and begins to flirt with the Bride.

If we begin to cultivate an attraction with the Bride, we have ceased to be the Bridegroom's friend and are now His adversary.

Jesus cares deeply enough for His friends that He will safeguard them from this pitfall. How? By making of them spiritual eunuchs who are safe company around His Bride.

I love the prayer of Jabez that has become popular among many today, "Lord, enlarge my territory" (see 1 Chronicles 4:10). It's a wonderful prayer when offered from a right spirit. But when prayed by someone who has been courting the Bride's favor, I can hear the King's response, "You have violated My territory already in the way you relate to My Bride. You've used what I've given you to promote your profile and popularity with her. I can't trust you with what you have; why should I give you more?"

THE USEFULNESS OF EUNUCHS

There is a kind of fierce allegiance to Jesus that relates to His Bride with absolute integrity and fearful honor. Eunuchs—true friends of the Bridegroom—are established in fiery allegiance to Jesus and are guarded in their relations with the Bride.

One reason this is so important is because of the power that is about to be released in the end-time church. The most glorious days of the church are immediately before us. God is going to establish His habitation among His people. The worship services will be explosively combustible. Healings and miracles will be medically verified and observable to all. Angelic activity will increase. People will come from long distances, and the meetings will go to arenas and stadiums and outdoor amphitheaters in order to accommodate the masses.

When Christ visits us with this kind of power and glory, and human leaders are used as the channels and conduits of Christ's blessings to the people, it's normal for the Bride to notice the leaders God is using most significantly. She can even become somewhat enamored with their giftings, insights, and platform anointing.

Therefore, before God can send the great outpouring of the last days, He must first prepare spiritual eunuchs in whom the issues of ambition, self-promotion, and desire for a public profile have been crucified.

The great longing of Jesus' true friends is that the name of Jesus be magnified in the earth. There's only one Name they desire to promote, and it's not their own.

Find a eunuch whose only ambition is that the Bride's affections for the Bridegroom be perfected, and you've found a vessel that can be trusted with an end-time anointing.

CHAPTER 8

THE WORSHIP INDUSTRY

All this talk of "spiritual eunuchs" and "hirelings" might seem a bit ethereal or theoretical, but I want to show how practical and relevant it truly is. Come with me, therefore, as we take the next three chapters to apply some of these principles specifically to those involved in the ministry of worship and the word.

If you serve in some way in the ministry of worship or the word, you share in something that is *especially* personal to Jesus. In the ministry of the word, Jesus washes and equips His Bride (Ephesians 4:12; 5:26). In the ministry of worship, He restores and invigorates His Bride. Little wonder, then, that these ministries are overseen by Jesus in a particularly attentive way.

Look at it this way: Pastors and worship leaders are engaging the mechanisms that shape the Bride's love exchange with the Bridegroom. In essence, we're stepping between the Potentate of the universe and His elect Bride and saying, "Here, let me help. Let me serve this love relationship. Jesus, I will help Your Bride love You with more extravagance and devotion. Church, I will help you understand who your

Beloved is, and will help you grow in the knowledge of His goodness and grace."

If we were not sovereignly *called* to such a ministry, it would seem frightfully presumptuous and absurdly preposterous for anyone to arrogate to himself the role of mediating the romance of the King of heaven with His Bride. The terribleness of the assignment makes the heart tremble.

Jesus doesn't need professional help with His love life. What He needs is true friends who will help Him by serving His Bride.

Only a fool stays in the ministry if he can get out. The only reason to stay in the ministry is because you're called and constrained. As the apostle Paul said, "For if I preach the gospel, I have nothing to boast of, for necessity is laid upon me; yes, woe is me if I do not preach the gospel!" (1 Corinthians 9:16). But if you can get out, get out. Be anything else, if you can. An administrator, a doctor, a bricklayer. Why? Because the area of worship is supervised by a Jealous Man. It's a fearful thing to lead worship because the King will hold you to close accounts for your stewardship.

Little wonder if you're feeling the fire of His jealousy in this moment; you've taken it upon yourself to minister to another Man's wife.

WORSHIP AND CHURCH GROWTH

The last thing you want to do is bring a business mentality to the ministry of worship.

When the Lord rebuked me for this, I had to confess that I had used worship to grow my ministry. I had used my God-given skills and anointing to create an atmosphere and culture conducive to corporate momentum and church growth. I thought I was doing it all just for Jesus, but the

Lord mercifully began to reveal to me how much I was invested in the thing. I had a whole lot of ownership. I was using worship for my own advantage. I had learned to draw from the Bride in order to fulfill my vision. I was becoming a ministry professional without realizing it.

I needed help for the thing to become personal again.

I had listened, you see, to the church growth consultants who said things like, "If you're wise and strategic, you can use preaching and worship to grow your church." His chastening hand in my life helped me to see that, in His eyes, worship isn't a tool for church growth. Worship isn't business, it's personal.

I've had to ask myself the tough questions. Is ministry something that enables me to expand my platform and public profile, enabling me to do greater exploits for God? Or is ministry something that I do out of personal loyalty to Jesus because He has called me as His bondservant? Is it personal for me, or is it business?

PROFESSIONALS

It's deadly when God's friends start to think and act like ministry professionals. When believers call us "Reverend," "Pastor," "Doctor," or "Bishop," we're a step away from seeing ourselves in a superior category. The spirit that overtook the ministry professionals of Jesus' day—the Pharisees—is as active today as it was then.

When God was preparing the planet for its greatest shift in all of history (I'm referring to the coming of Jesus, the Baby, to earth), not a solitary pastor or clergyman tuned into what God was doing. The professionals were utterly oblivious to the fact that a virgin was pregnant with the Messiah. It didn't even appear as the tiniest blip on their screens. Pharisees, scribes, elders—none of them was in a place spiritually to pick up a clue. Those who should have gotten it didn't. Who picked it up? A no-name, no-title man and woman named Simeon and Anna who were ablaze with a spirit of prayer.

Leadership positions can actually distract us from the very sensitivity we are thought to be maintaining. We can become so preoccupied with serving the Bride that we neglect our vital connection to the Bridegroom.

We live in an age when the driving agenda of so many ministers, in its raw essence, is a relationship with the Bride. They spend more energy investing in a relationship with the Bride than with the Bridegroom.

I once heard an apostolic leader, while addressing pastors in a training session, commend his practices with this statement, "I never read the Bible just for myself. I've moved past that. I come to the word so that I might feed others."

At first glance, that practice might appear as a selfless concern for others. But a paradigm of spiritual leadership that gives more attention to the body than to the Head is bankrupt. It's true that leaders need to be faithful to feed the flock of God; but the only way to be a true witness for Jesus is to come to the word for yourself first, and then feed the flock from the overflow of what the Holy Spirit is speaking to you personally.

The true friend of the Bridegroom doesn't come to the word primarily to find sermon material but to see the Living Word in the pages that point to Him. He knows he will effectively serve the Bride only to the degree that he is maintaining a fiery, intimate relationship with the Bridegroom.

The great leaders of this end-time generation will be those who have a personal, compelling relationship with Jesus, and who come to the word primarily for the purpose of encountering the Man, Jesus Christ. If you don't demonstrate a compelling passion for Jesus in this hour, you will be bypassed as worthy to help the Bride prepare herself for her wedding day.

IS WORSHIP AN INDUSTRY TO YOU?

Back in the mid-1980s, I was on the teaching faculty of an event called the "Worship Symposium." It was there I was introduced to a fledgling ministry that had a vision to produce cassettes of "live" congregational worship. The Holy Spirit was breathing fresh life into the worship of the church, and this tape ministry came onto the scene at just the right time to fan the flame. It equipped the Bride of Christ with new songs that facilitated the dynamic spirit of praise and worship erupting in the earth.

At first, the only way to get their new releases was by direct mail-order. At the time, the contemporary Christian music industry looked at the idea with skepticism. "You mean, you're going to record congregational singing, led by a worship leader, put it on a cassette, and expect people to *buy* it?" Nobody carried the tapes because nobody thought they would sell. Considering what typical congregational worship was like in 1984, the idea did seem far-fetched. At the time, congregational worship was more often something to be endured than recorded.

But when people listened to their recordings, they had an immediate connection with the passion, freshness, energy, and simplicity of devotion to Christ that the recordings demonstrated. Unlike the direction the contemporary Christian music industry had taken, these recordings were not personality driven. They exalted Jesus.

That company's mail-order business exploded. Everybody seemed to want those tapes. You couldn't find them in Christian bookstores, so churches bought them in quantity and sold them directly to their congregation. Sales were stunning.

It wasn't too long before the marketers caught on, however, and soon worship cassettes began to appear on the shelves of the nation's bookstores. Managers were suddenly realizing there was money to be made. At first they were placed in a corner on a shelf, but soon they were given prime store displays because of the burgeoning demand. Other ministries began producing worship tapes around the same period of time, so the breadth of the selections expanded.

Back then, I always looked forward to receiving my new worship tape in the mail. A new one came every two months, and I would eagerly listen to it as soon as I received it.

I remember one particular day in the early 1990s, getting my new worship tape in the mail and eagerly plugging it into my tape deck to see what new songs had been produced. I hit the play button, and the first sound I heard on the recording was, "Ladies and gentlemen"—followed by the name of the worship leader (who, by the way, is a wonderful brother in Christ). I felt like I'd been hit in the chest. It was now about a personality. In that moment I realized the worship movement had become an industry.

My point is not how bad we all are. My point is this: God catapulted the worship movement onto the world stage through nameless servants who had an authentic heart cry to glorify the name of Christ. We've lost some of the early purity of the movement, but I'm not discouraged, God will return us to the zeal of our beginnings. I'm convinced God is going to both restore purity of heart to the worship movement and take us to even greater heights of consecration. Our God, whose name is Jealous, will do it.

God is about to take worship to a whole new level. And when He does, He won't use the marketers and merchandisers. He'll use those with a spirit of meekness whose hearts burn for the Lord Jesus Christ and yearn for His return. He's going to use those for whom the honor of Jesus' name is a personal matter.

When the last great move of the Holy Spirit comes upon the earth, I don't want to be found among the marketers—capitalizing on the Holy Spirit's momentum in order to strengthen sales. I want to be among those who are facedown in the presence of the majestic, beautiful King.

CHAPTER 9

THREE PARADIGMS
OF WORSHIP

I closed out Chapter 7 by pointing to the glory that is coming to the church. I want to expand upon that even further.

It's essential that we have both a clear expectation regarding the great end-time harvest of souls that will precede Christ's second coming, as well as a sober realization of how important it is to God that His servants be prepared properly to provide effective leadership in that hour of visitation.

When we consider the severity of God in making spiritual eunuchs, we might be tempted to complain, "Lord, You're being overly harsh. Your knife doesn't need to be this severe in order for me to respond to You. You're not just refining me, You're killing me."

If you're ever tempted to think God is over-pruning you, you're not alone. The strength of God's disciplines in the lives of His servants makes sense, however, only when we have an accurate perspective on the visitation that's coming. Very soon now, God is going to visit His church in such a way that crowds are going to mushroom, offerings are going to skyrocket, miracles are going to abound, and

the momentum ministries will experience will be unprecedented. If we haven't been adequately pruned and tested
in the lean times, the coming glory will have the potential
to destroy us.

The leaders who will be useful in the Master's hand in
that hour are eunuchs who have had cut away from their
lives every self-serving interest, and who are available to
Jesus simply because of their personal devotion to Him.

With that in view, I would like to paint a picture of
where I see God taking the worshiping church in the days
ahead. To do that, I'll begin by surveying where we've come
from.

PRELIMINARIES

Let me go back to my childhood for a moment. Back
in the 1960s, the church was largely functioning in a "preliminaries" paradigm of worship. Most services had just two
elements to them: preliminaries and the sermon. Everything
in a meeting prior to the sermon was "preliminary" to the
sermon. The sermon was the main event. Everything leading up to it was secondary. The preliminaries, therefore,
were things like worship, prayer, readings, Communion,
announcements, offering, baby dedications, special music,
etc. Worship was one of several preliminaries.

Not that worship wasn't important. It was. It just wasn't
as important as the preaching of the word.

The following example illustrates the priorities of that
era. In the church tradition in which I grew up, there was
one general qualification for being a worship leader. Did
they ask if you could sing? No, that wasn't the question.
Did they ask if you were a musician? No, that wasn't the
necessary qualification to lead worship. Did they ask if you
had the heart of a worshiper? No. The main question asked

of those leading worship was this: Are you on the board? If you were a board member, that meant you would be asked to lead worship. It doubled as a platform to give the board members greater visibility in the congregation.

A lot of things have changed. Now we have worship leaders in paid salary positions at many churches, something that wasn't even in the imagination of pastors back in the 1960s.

PRESENCE

Then something happened. A move of the Spirit took place in America in the 1970s, often dubbed the Charismatic Renewal. With it came not only a glorious wave of anointed teaching but also a glorious renewal in worship.

Perhaps the most outstanding revelation of worship in that day was the awakening of the church to the implications of Psalm 22:3, "But thou art holy, O thou that inhabitest the praises of Israel." (I'm quoting the King James Version because it was the primary translation used back then.) The message exploded across the body of Christ that God inhabits the praises of His people. When we praise Him, He responds by establishing His presence among His people.

This emphasis moved the church into an entirely fresh dimension of worship, which I call the "presence" paradigm of worship. Worship, we realized, is our way into the presence of God. When the power of praise and worship gripped the church, we changed the way we ran our services because we recognized there was not just one main event in a service, but *two*. Worship and the word took on equal significance.

We began to consider that a worship service deserved the same investment in planning and preparation as the sermon. A pastor didn't just "throw together" a sermon on

Sunday morning; neither should a worship leader, then, "throw together" a worship service at last minute.

That's when worship teams began to form—teams that gathered at another time in the week to pray together and practice. New levels of commitment began to produce new levels of excellence in the musical expressions of our worship that is still growing to this day.

The presence paradigm of worship totally over-ran the preliminaries paradigm, and took the nations and denominations by storm. We're over 30 years into it now, and this remains the universal paradigm of worship in the church today. The saints gather on Sunday morning, we lift up songs of praise, and we expect God to presence Himself in our midst. After the meeting, everyone goes home, tackles their week, and then we gather together again the following Sunday, at which time we start all over to invoke the presence of God through praise and worship. Every time we gather, it's as though we're starting from scratch because of the extended periods of time between meetings.

We are not going to be staying forever, however, in the presence paradigm. In fact, I'm sensing that time is just about up, and the Lord is right now in the process of transitioning us to something new.

HABITATION

There is a day coming—very soon—when God is going to break us out of the confines of the presence paradigm and catapult us into the fullness of what has been in His heart all along. I call it the habitation paradigm of worship.

Habitation is the word I'm using to describe what Paul talked about in Ephesians 2:21-22:

> *In whom the whole building, being fitted together,*
> *grows into a holy temple in the Lord, in whom you*
> *also are being built together for a dwelling place of*
> *God in the Spirit.*

God's purpose all along has been that the church be His dwelling place. God doesn't want to simply visit with His people once a week; He wants to establish His habitation among them and abide with them. He wants a 24/7 burning reality of continual fellowship with the saints on earth, just as He has with the saints in heaven. He wants worship "'on earth as it is in heaven'" (Matthew 6:10). Incessant, extravagant, abandoned worship.

The start/stop/start/stop model is finished. Ninety-minute Christianity is over. God is establishing the church in this hour as a 24/7 house of prayer because He wants to visit us with habitation.

Amos foretold this was coming when he wrote, "'On that day I will raise up the tabernacle of David, which has fallen down, and repair its damages; I will raise up its ruins, and rebuild it as in the days of old'" (Amos 9:11). He was referring to the pattern of 24/7 worship inaugurated by David. David established round-the-clock worship and praise in Zion thousands of years ago because he had a vision for habitation. David knew that God is surrounded by unceasing thanksgiving and praise, and he knew that we would not see the habitation of God on earth until there is established for Him a resting place of incessant, affectionate thanksgiving and praise.

Beloved, God's not downsizing to shorter services; He's upgrading to 24/7.

When habitation comes, the meeting never stops. Because when God is in the house, no one wants to leave. You can shut off the lights and power down the sound system, but if God's in the house, you can't get the people to leave. The meeting keeps going. Some might leave briefly for other necessary duties, but they're soon back. In all the coming and going, the meeting continues seamlessly as the glory of God is manifest among His people.

This is what happened in the wilderness when the multitudes had Jesus in their presence. It was so glorious to be with Him that they never left; they just camped out. Never mind that they had no food, they were with Jesus. After three days of that, Jesus had to forcefully close down the meeting and retreat to the mountain because if He had stayed they would have stayed too. The people were basking in the glory of habitation and they didn't want it to stop.

Habitation simply means that God is there, and that He is demonstrating His presence with tangible manifestations of power and glory.

Some churches are trimming back their worship time to get more people into their building. But in a day when the Holy Spirit is trying to coach the church into 24/7, I don't want to be found pushing in the opposite direction for "leaner and tighter."

Some pastoral teams are wrestling with the question, "How can we take what we do in 90 minutes, trim away the fat, and deliver the same punch in 75 minutes?" The thinking is that shorter meetings make our services more palatable and relevant to seekers and non-believers. I love the desire to be reaching the non-churched; but our fundamental problem in America is not a lack of people in our meetings. Our problem is, we need God in our meetings!

Under the guise of "reaching for the harvest," we have validated a professional model of ministry, led by hirelings, that uses astute business practices to gain favor with the

Bride. We're exuberant because we're now hearing the voice of the Bride (growing attendance), rather than heartsick with longing to hear the voice of the Bridegroom. Where are the friends of the Bridegroom who burn for His agenda and not their own?

I've come to the brilliant conclusion that people are fundamentally boring. So if you get 300 people in a building, you have boring times 300. If you get 3,000 people in a building, you have boring times 3,000.

Get God in your building—now you've got something!

Now, I realize that the fullness of habitation will not happen until the age to come. The fullness that we long for is expressed in Revelation 21:3.

> *And I heard a loud voice from heaven saying, "Behold, the tabernacle of God is with men, and He will dwell with them, and they shall be His people. God Himself will be with them and be their God."*

When God tabernacles among His people in that manner, O what glory we will behold! In that day, we will experience the fullness of what it means to have God's habitation among men. The Father will actually bring heaven to earth and establish His eternal residence on the earth with us!

I realize we're not going to experience that level of glory in this age. We will, however, experience down-payments of that fullness in this age, according to the manifold wisdom and grace of God. What God reveals in fullness in the age to come He reveals now in incremental ways because He is the same yesterday, today, and forever (Hebrews 13:8).

Abba Father, how much more will You give us? Grant us as much of Yourself as our human spirit can sustain in our current limitations. We want You!

CHAPTER 10

THE GLORY
OF HABITATION

So, what *will* it look like when God establishes His habitation in the midst of His people? Paul pointed to the glory of that reality when he described normative corporate worship under the grace of the New Covenant.

> *But if all prophesy, and an unbeliever or an uninformed person comes in, he is convinced by all, he is convicted by all. And thus the secrets of his heart are revealed; and so, falling down on his face, he will worship God and report that God is truly among you* (1 Corinthians 14:24-25).

When God is resident in the house at this level of glory, almost everyone at the meeting is profoundly aware of God's immediate presence. Even the unbelievers are gripped with the fact that God is among His people.

One primary way the unbeliever or uninformed person is made aware of God being present is through the spiritual gift of prophecy. When the Holy Spirit reveals the secrets of an unbeliever's heart in public, He doesn't do so by exposing his sins; rather, He identifies the innermost longings of his heart. The unbeliever suddenly realizes, "God knows me! He knows my address; he knows my thoughts; he knows my desires and dreams. God is right here, in this place!" Conviction descends upon him and he falls on his face, worshiping God.

When was the last time you had an unbeliever fall on his face in one of your worship services? It happens quite rarely in our current presence model, but when habitation comes, get ready. Sinners will be falling on their faces and crying out because even hardened, cynical, crusty sinners will acknowledge that the Almighty God of the universe is resident among His people.

Paul went on to say that the unbeliever will "report that God is truly among you." He'll go home and tell his family and friends, "Guys, I thought I was just going to a church service. But when I got there, God was there! It scared me to death! He stopped the whole service to talk to *me*. Wow, was that ever intense. He used exact phrases I had spoken just this morning. It's true, God really *does* know every word we speak and every thought we think. I'm still trembling all over. I'm telling you, if you want to meet up with God, go to that place. God is there!"

It's not so hard to get a meeting hot enough that the fiery *believers* who were there leave the meeting talking energetically about it; but when stone-cold *unbelievers* leave the meeting saying, "God was there!" now you've got something.

When God establishes His habitation among His people, it hardly matters in what condition you come to the meeting, you will be impacted by God's presence. You might be mad, sad, or glad. You might be bored, angry, critical, distracted, engaged, cold, or hot. Regardless of your emotional frame, when the glory of God is being manifest, you will be deeply aware that you are in no typical worship service. God is in the house.

THE COMING GLORY

I'm emphasizing right now that God is getting ready to take corporate worship to a whole new level. We've been in unbelief so long we can't even believe the glory of God is going to come into the assembly. But what Joel prophesied is coming (Joel 2:28-32). The Spirit is going to be poured out on all flesh in an unprecedented manner. He has already poured out His Spirit to a certain degree (for which we are grateful), but a greater measure of outpouring is about to come upon us.

When God comes in habitation, our buildings will not be able to contain the harvest. The meetings will go the stadiums of the earth, and people will come from all over to meet up with God. For brief periods of time, football stadiums will become houses of prayer.

One of the things that will attend the coming glory will be a greater release of angelic activity among God's people, in accordance with their scriptural assignment: "Are they not all ministering spirits sent forth to minister for those who will inherit salvation?" (Hebrews 1:14).

PRAISE ANGELS

I believe the day is closely upon us when angels will once again get involved in our worship gatherings. You might ask, "'Once again?' Have they ever been involved in corporate worship?" I think the answer is, "Yes."

When the host of angels announced Christ's birth to the shepherds, they spoke a refrain that is gripping in its uniqueness. It had never been uttered previously in Scripture:

> *"Glory to God in the highest, and on earth peace,*
> *goodwill toward men!"* (Luke 2:14).

It was an angelic chorus, and the only other time it was verbalized in Scripture appears to have been equally empowered by angelic activity. I'm referring to the triumphal entry of Christ into Jerusalem, when the multitudes lifted their voices in praise to God with remarkably similar words, saying, "'Peace in heaven and glory in the highest!'" (Luke 19:38).

If you've never thought of angels being present and active at the triumphal entry, a review of the account might help you to see it.

> *Then, as He was now drawing near the descent of the*
> *Mount of Olives, the whole multitude of the disciples*
> *began to rejoice and praise God with a loud voice for*
> *all the mighty works they had seen, saying: "'Blessed is*
> *the King who comes in the name of the LORD!' Peace*
> *in heaven and glory in the highest!" And some of the*
> *Pharisees called to Him from the crowd, "Teacher, rebuke*
> *Your disciples." But He answered and said to them, "I*
> *tell you that if these should keep silent, the stones would*
> *immediately cry out"* (Luke 19:37-40).

Talk about a worship service with crowd momentum, this event had it! Matthew reported that "all the city was moved" (Matthew 21:10). The energy on the praise was so tangible that some of the Pharisees, in alarm over where the crowd momentum could lead, urged Jesus to stop the whole thing.

When you think about it, there was no natural reason for this praise service to have this kind of energy on it. I mean, look at the dynamics involved. For starters, it was an outdoor venue. If anyone reading this has ever tried to lead worship in an outdoor venue, you know how difficult it is. There are no walls to reflect the voices back to the worshipers, and when people don't have an awareness of others singing around them, they naturally lower their voices themselves. It's extremely difficult to cultivate a corporate sound of praise in an outdoor setting.

Furthermore, they had no sound system. An outdoor worship concert is doable with a strong sound system, but with no sound system to carry the worship team, it becomes virtually impossible.

But this event had even more strikes against it. There was no worship leader. No one had planned for it, no one had selected any songs to sing, and no one was providing leadership to the multitude.

Add to that the fact that there were no musical instruments being played. No mics, no sound amplification, no singers, no musicians, no leader, no planning, no acoustical reinforcement. Add it up and you come to only one conclusion: This worship service was doomed to abysmal failure from the start. And as though all that weren't tough enough, there were scowling Pharisees, like wet blankets, trying to smother the thing with their indignation and displeasure.

And yet, in spite of all the natural hindrances, the praise was explosive. The atmosphere was so combustible that Jesus Himself said, "'I tell you that if these should keep silent, the stones would immediately cry out.'" What caused such a dynamic eruption of praise under seemingly impossible circumstances? There is only one reasonable answer: angels. Praise angels. I'm suggesting that angels were igniting the words that were being spoken ("'Peace in heaven and glory in the highest!'"), and they were empowering the multitude with a spirit of praise. The spiritual energy being released was so strong that, had the people shut their mouths, the very rocks would have cried out. (Rocks only cry out under supernatural power.)

A PERSONAL EXPERIENCE WITH ANGELIC ACTIVITY

I remember a meeting in which I touched a measure of this reality. The year was 1986. I was a 29-year-old pastor/worship leader at the time and was asked to pull together a worship team for the annual pastors' conference of my denomination. I was looking forward to the ministry of our guest speaker because I had heard a lot about him but had never been in a meeting with him. His name was John Wimber, and he was known to be gifted in activating believers in the ministry of healing.

I still remember the first night of that conference. The place was electric. You could almost hear the crackling of charged particles in the atmosphere. The spirit of expectation in the house was contagious. When I hit the first chord on the piano, the building exploded. We were immediately at 36,000 feet. No runway, no lift-off, no ascending curve, we were instantly in the stratosphere. At the throne. To a twenty-something worship leader, the adrenalin of the moment was a rush.

I was like a teenager behind the wheel of a super-charged sports car. One little nudge on the accelerator and the engine would roar to life. The feeling of power was unbelievable. As a worship leader, I realized in that moment it was almost impossible to take a wrong turn. It felt like I could pull just about any song out of the bag and it would work. Hit a note on the piano, that was sufficient. They didn't even need a song. Simply hit a note and we were at 36,000 feet.

The power I felt in that moment, frankly, was intoxicating. I held the worship service in my hands, and it was going to be off the charts no matter what song I sang. I kept telling myself that the energy of the meeting was not my doing. "I know there's more going on here than just my leadership." Even so, I couldn't shut off the instinctive thoughts, "I must admit, however, that the leaders of this conference were certainly wise when they asked *me* to lead the worship this year." I couldn't help it, something inside was subconsciously taking partial credit for the tremendous success of the worship service.

I have a lot more objectivity about it now. Now, more than twenty years later, I realize the energy on that worship gathering had absolutely nothing to do with me and my "awesome leadership giftings." What was the cause? Angels. I realize it now: John Wimber had a cadre of angels following him around in that season wherever he went. The angels got involved in the praises, and in the healings (John 5:4), and in whatever ways the Lord intended them to serve the saints (Hebrews 1:14). And it was powerful.

There I was, a young buck, sitting at the console of the piano and feeling the power of the engine. I wasn't properly prepared to steward the anointing of that moment. Although I was singing all the right words to Jesus, something about that moment was selfishly about me. My heart wanted it to be personal between me and Jesus, but in the euphoria of the moment it became business. I was aware of how competent I was appearing.

Now I'm finally getting to my point. When the glory of God is manifest in worship, as He has promised to us, it will be tempting for leaders to use the platform visibility and name recognition of that moment for personal advantage. Our only safety will be if we have been tested in the crucible and prepared by the Lord to handle that kind of attention with maturity.

Our most glorious days are before us. God will establish His habitation among His people; the glory of God will be tangibly demonstrated in the church; angelic activity will escalate; miracles will take place, together with signs and wonders; a spirit of prophecy will rest upon the church; our buildings will not be able to accommodate the press of the people, and this move of God will go to the stadiums of the earth. Who will provide leadership in such an hour? Those for whom the whole thing has become intensely personal between them and Jesus. This kind of glory is safe only for true friends of the Bridegroom.

THE SOBRIETY OF WHAT'S COMING

Every one of us longs for the coming glory. We cry out for it. We long to see the glory of His face and the power of His hand demonstrated in the earth in the sight of the nations.

However, there is a fearful side to this thing. What is fearful is the preparatory process God will take us through to make us worthy vessels to steward such glory.

To become a friend of the Bridegroom, as John the Baptist was, requires a stint in the wilderness.

> He said: "I am 'The voice of one crying in the wilderness: "Make straight the way of the LORD,"'" as the prophet Isaiah said" (John 1:23).

Never married, John the Baptist served Jesus much like a eunuch in the courts of the King. In John's terminology, he called himself "the friend of the Bridegroom." We could just as well use the term, "a spiritual eunuch." Both terms refer to the same reality: a personal loyalty to the King that selflessly serves His interests.

Whatever severe means God must use to get us there (be it a wilderness or a knife), may we be qualified as fitting carriers of His glory in the hour of His visitation.

CHAPTER 11

THE CROSS MAKES
IT PERSONAL

W hen God first calls us to serve Him, we launch out with sincerity, humility, meekness, lovesickness, and purity of heart. However, most of us tend to collect stuff over time. What starts off in simplicity of heart often gets cluttered with professionalism, seniority, promotion, and entitlement. We have a way, in our carnality, of getting over into a business mode—and it can happen so subtly and slowly that we don't even catch it.

God has a way, however, of keeping things personal. When God applies the cross to your life, you can't help but take it personally.

When King Nebuchadnezzar made a eunuch of Daniel, you can be sure Daniel took it personally.

When Candace made a eunuch of her Treasurer, he took it personally.

When God allowed Job's ten children to be killed, Job took it personally.

When God took out Jacob's hip, it was personal.

When the Father crucified the Son, Jesus took it personally.

Sometimes God does things in our lives that make everything about our relationship with Him extremely personal.

CRUCIFIXION IS A PERSONAL THING

When I see leaders in the body of Christ with a business mentality, I don't fret because I'm aware God knows how to make it personal. He can bring a cross into your life at any time. If this thing has become business for you, the kindest thing He can do is impale you to a cross.

The cross has a way of knocking the business clean out of you. When impaled to a cross, your business chip gets crushed.

The cross is God's way of making things personal.

When Jesus did the cross, the whole thing became intensely personal for Him. When men railed on Him, He realized their hatred was personal. When the hordes of hell pounced on Him, He took their rage personally. When the Father forsook Him, He took it personally.

When someone puts nails in your hands and feet, you take it personally. "They're doing this to *me*. They're coming against *me*."

When God strikes you (Ezekiel 7:9), take it personally.

RESURRECTION IS A PERSONAL THING

When God rescues you from your pit, go ahead and take it personally.

When God delivered David, he took it personally: "He delivered me because He delighted in me" (Psalm 18:19).

When God resurrected Jesus, He was making a personal statement about His delight in His Son. That's what Romans 1:4 is pointing to when it says that Jesus was "declared to be the Son of God with power…by the resurrection from the dead." By resurrecting Him the Father was declaring Jesus to be the Son of God.

Acts 13:33 confirms this, indicating that when the Father resurrected the Son, He actually announced aloud in Hades, "'You are My Son, today I have begotten You.'" Hell must have shaken at the sound! Everyone in hell knew, in that moment, how the Father felt about His Son. Little wonder Jesus took His resurrection personally.

IT WAS PERSONAL FOR JOB

Job was a man in the Bible who experienced both crucifixion and resurrection. He is best known for the great cross he bore. Through divinely orchestrated events, He lost all his possessions and livelihood (his servants and sheep were killed, and his donkeys, camels, and oxen were stolen from him). Then, in the same day, he lost all ten of his children to a natural disaster ("a whirlwind"). Later, he lost his health to a plague of boils that covered his body. The most godly man alive at the time was suddenly suffering the most of any man alive.

The reason Job was suffering so intensely was because of a wager that God had going with the devil. Satan had accused Job to God with an argument that was essentially like this: "Job serves You because of how You bless His life. He's not in it for You; he's in it for Your blessings. It's not personal to him, it's business. Let me sift him and You'll see what I mean. He'll show his true colors. Take your blessing off his business and I bet he'll curse You to Your face!" (I am loosely interpreting Job 1:9-11.)

God believed that Job was in it, ultimately, for personal reasons, so He accepted Satan's wager. "I bet he'll still love Me, Satan, even if you hit his business." God allowed Satan to strike Job's possessions, plunging Job's world suddenly into chaos and calamity.

Job was an astute businessman, but when God took Job's business down, the whole thing suddenly became intensely personal for him. He realized, "God hit *me*. He took *me* out. His discipline is upon *me*."

When God places you between a rock and a hard place, where nothing or nobody but He can help or deliver you, it has a way of making everything personal. "No one else can help me, God; it's just You and me now. You're my only hope."

I can imagine someone coming to Job after God struck his business and saying, "Job, I feel terrible, this is awful what has happened to you. But since you've lost all your livelihood and source of income, don't you think you should try your hand at something else? I mean, you still have to provide for your wife. Isn't it time to get off this ash heap and start putting some energy into cultivating a stream of income?"

Job would likely respond, "I've had the business knocked right out of me. This isn't about business anymore. This is personal. It's personal between me and God. So I'm going to stay on this ash heap until He talks to me!"

Life had come to a screeching halt, and now Job wanted only one thing: an audience with the King.

When God wounds you, He means for you to take it personally. It really is all about you and Him. You find yourself looking at God and saying, "God, I want to talk about You and me. You. And me. Where are we at? What are You thinking when You look at me? I've lost my bearings on our relationship. My emotions are telling me You're angry with me. I need to hear it directly from You. Talk to me. What's up with You and me?"

"MY SERVANT JOB"

The final chapter of the Book of Job gives us some insight on how things ended between Job and God. Here's an excerpt from that closing chapter.

And so it was, after the LORD had spoken these words to Job, that the LORD said to Eliphaz the Temanite, "My wrath is aroused against you and your two friends, for you have not spoken of Me what is right, as My servant Job has. Now therefore, take for yourselves seven bulls and seven rams, go to My servant Job, and offer up for yourselves a burnt offering; and My servant Job shall pray for you. For I will accept him, lest I deal with you according to your folly; because you have not spoken of Me what is right, as My servant Job has." So Eliphaz the Temanite and Bildad the Shuhite and Zophar the Naamathite went and did as the LORD commanded them; for the LORD had accepted Job. And the LORD restored Job's losses when he prayed for his friends. Indeed the LORD gave Job twice as much as he had before" (Job 42:7-10).

I hear Eliphaz saying to Job, "Job, I'm terrified! God just talked to me, and I'm scared out of my wits."

I suppose Job replying with, "Well, good. I'm glad I'm not the only one. It's kind of refreshing, actually, to hear that somebody else is also terrified of Him."

Eliphaz continues, "I'm absolutely serious. I'm shaken and undone. God said He's angry with me and Bildad and Zophar because we haven't spoken rightly of Him, like you have. And he said that if you don't pray for us, He'll deal with us according to our folly. Job, I'm petrified! Please, please, please pray for us!"

That part of the conversation is essentially present in the text. Now, I'd like to suggest a hypothetical conversation that isn't present in the text, but which could have potentially happened.

I can imagine Job responded to Eliphaz's plea by saying, "Sure, Eliphaz. I'll pray for you. I'd be glad to. But before we do that, could I ask just one question?"

Eliphaz came back, "Certainly. What would you like to know?"

"When God talked to you," Job wondered, "did He say my name?"

Eliphaz paused at the unusual question. "Well...actually, yes."

"He said my name!" exclaimed Job.

"Yes," affirmed Eliphaz. "He said the name, 'Job.' But that's not all, He said more. His actual words were, 'My servant Job.'"

Job questioned him eagerly on that. "He called me His servant?"

"Yes," Eliphaz replied, locking on Job's gaze. "He said you were His servant. And He said it four times."

At that, Job looked down and stepped back. His throat was tight. "Okay," he finally managed, his eyes lifting to the horizon as though seeing something afar off. "Thanks, Eliphaz. That's all I wanted to know." Absorbed in his thoughts, he turned and slowly walked away.

He said my name! That was enough for Job. All he cared about, after coming through something so agonizing and intense, was that at the end of it God owned him.

SAY MY NAME

If you're one of God's friends, He may take you through a crucible similar to Job's—an intense, eunuch-kind-ofcutting-away, in which the business is knocked out of you and everything becomes personal between you and God. The true friends of the Bridegroom have persevered through the test and proven their personal allegiance to the Bridegroom.

Your journey might include a great crushing and a great death. But the story of God's servant is not complete until crucifixion is followed with resurrection. The story, properly written, ends with the hearts of the Bridegroom and His Bride sealed in fiery intimacy.

God had crushed Job to make it personal for *him;* then He raised him up because it was personal for *Him.*

His ways remain unchanged. He'll crush you because He wants it to be personal for you; then He'll raise you up to demonstrate His delight in you.

Abba, I believe I can endure this present distress if only, in the end, You'll say my name and own me as Your son. This cross has made it personal for me. My soul will be at rest when You demonstrate with Your resurrection power that our relationship has become equally personal for You.

For descriptions on all of Bob's titles,
please visit *www.oasishouse.net*.

Order Form
Books by Bob Sorge

	Qty.	Price	Total
BOOKS:			
IT'S NOT BUSINESS, IT'S PERSONAL		$ 9.00	
POWER OF THE BLOOD: Approaching God With Confidence		$12.00	
UNRELENTING PRAYER		$12.00	
ENVY: THE ENEMY WITHIN		$12.00	
LOYALTY: The Reach of the Noble Heart		$13.00	
FOLLOWING THE RIVER: A Vision for Corporate Worship		$ 9.00	
SECRETS OF THE SECRET PLACE		$14.00	
Secrets Of The Secret Place COMPANION Study Guide		$10.00	
GLORY: When Heaven Invades Earth		$ 9.00	
PAIN, PERPLEXITY & PROMOTION		$13.00	
THE FIRE OF GOD'S LOVE		$12.00	
THE FIRE OF DELAYED ANSWERS		$13.00	
IN HIS FACE: A Prophetic Call to Renewed Focus		$12.00	
EXPLORING WORSHIP: A Practical Guide to Praise and Worship		$15.00	
Exploring Worship WORKBOOK & DISCUSSION GUIDE		$ 5.00	
DEALING WITH THE REJECTION AND PRAISE OF MAN		$ 9.00	

SPECIAL PACKET
Buy one each of all Bob's books, and save 30%.
Call or visit our website for a current price.

Subtotal	
Shipping, Add 10% (Minimum of $3.00)	
Missouri Residents Add 7.6% Sales Tax	
Total Enclosed	

U.S. Funds Only

Send payment with order to: Oasis House
PO Box 522
Grandview, MO 64030-0522

Name _____

Address: Street _____

City _____ State _____

Zip _____

For quantity discounts and MasterCard/VISA or international orders, call
816-767-8880 or order on our fully secure website: www.oasishouse.net.
See our site for free sermon downloads.